EXPLORATION THROUGH THE AGES

THE VOYAGES OF VASCO DA GAMA

Richard Humble

Illustrated by
Doug Harker and Francis Phillipps

Franklin Watts
New York · London · Toronto · Sydney

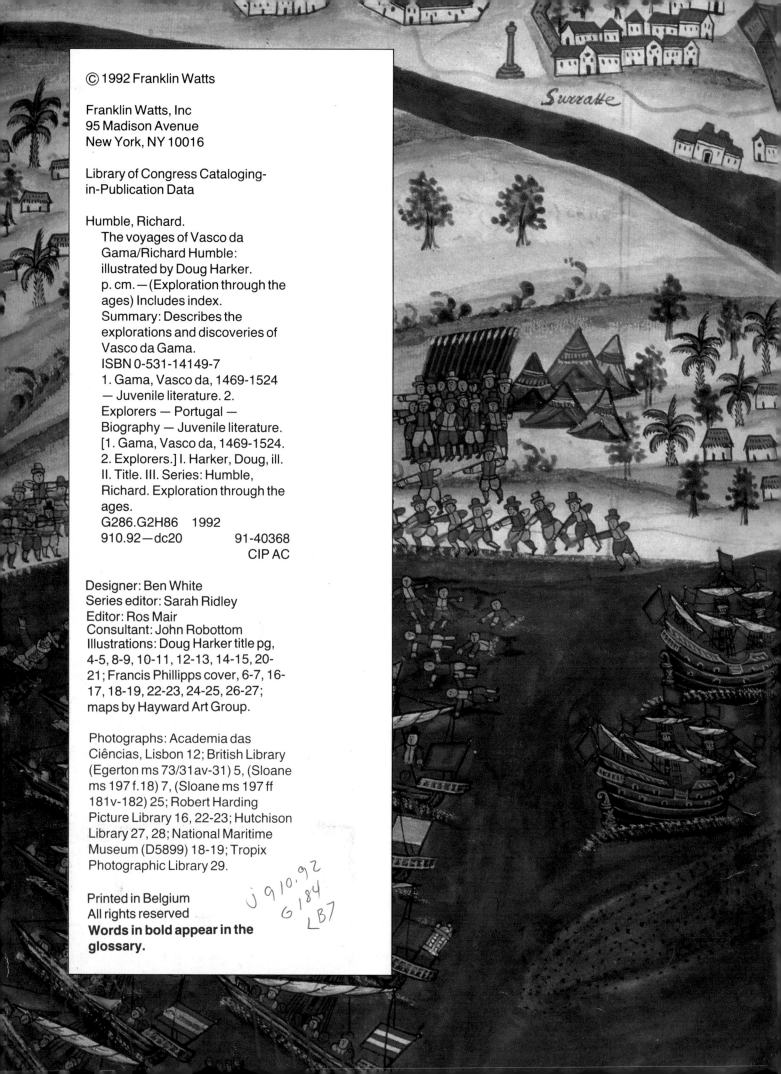

Franklin Watts, Inc
95 Madison Avenue
New York, NY 10016

Library of Congress Cataloging-
in-Publication Data

Humble, Richard.
    The voyages of Vasco da
    Gama/Richard Humble:
    illustrated by Doug Harker.
    p. cm. — (Exploration through the
    ages) Includes index.
    Summary: Describes the
    explorations and discoveries of
    Vasco da Gama.
    ISBN 0-531-14149-7
    1. Gama, Vasco da, 1469-1524
    — Juvenile literature. 2.
    Explorers — Portugal —
    Biography — Juvenile literature.
    [1. Gama, Vasco da, 1469-1524.
    2. Explorers.] I. Harker, Doug, ill.
    II. Title. III. Series: Humble,
    Richard. Exploration through the
    ages.
    G286.G2H86   1992
    910.92—dc20   91-40368
                         CIP AC

Designer: Ben White
Series editor: Sarah Ridley
Editor: Ros Mair
Consultant: John Robottom
Illustrations: Doug Harker title pg,
4-5, 8-9, 10-11, 12-13, 14-15, 20-
21; Francis Phillipps cover, 6-7, 16-
17, 18-19, 22-23, 24-25, 26-27;
maps by Hayward Art Group.

Photographs: Academia das
Ciências, Lisbon 12; British Library
(Egerton ms 73/31av-31) 5, (Sloane
ms 197 f.18) 7, (Sloane ms 197 ff
181v-182) 25; Robert Harding
Picture Library 16, 22-23; Hutchison
Library 27, 28; National Maritime
Museum (D5899) 18-19; Tropix
Photographic Library 29.

Contents

Sea route to India

Just over 500 years ago, in 1488, two small sailing ships from Portugal made one of the most important sea voyages in the history of the world. They ventured thousands of miles further south than any ship had dared before. These two ships, under their commander Bartolomeo Diaz, were the first to sail from Europe around Africa's southern tip and enter the Indian Ocean.

Leaving a column topped by a cross to mark the furthest point reached along the south African coast, Diaz and his men turned west and north for home, over 11,250 kilometers (7,000 miles) away. They arrived back at Lisbon in Decembe

▷ The voyages of the Portuguese explorers Diogo Cao and Bartolomeo Diaz, made on the orders of King John II of Portugal between 1483 and 1488. These voyages used small, light ships known as **caravels,** ideal for following unknown coasts in often shallow and dangerous waters. Among their stores they carried specially made stone columns. A column, or *padrao*, was set up on high ground as a landmark for the crews who would follow in future years. After Cao had mapped 2,330 kilometers (1,450 miles) of previously unknown west African coastline, Diaz rounded the Cape of Good Hope into the Indian Ocean in January 1488, setting up a *padrao* before returning to the Atlantic and home.

▽ Signpost to India: the lone *padrao* planted on the south African coast as the caravels of Diaz head for home in March 1488.

EUROPE

PORTUGAL
Lisbon

Madeira Islands

MUSLIM WORLD

Cape Verde Islands

Elmina

INDIA

AFRICA

Cape of Good Hope

Muslim World, 1488

Lands mapped by Portugal, 1488

Diogo Cao, 1482-4, 1485-6

Bartolomeo Diaz 1487-88

1488 with the news that the southern end of Africa had been found and passed by sea. The ocean route from Europe around Africa to the rich markets of India and China now lay open.

By 1488, the Portuguese had built up more skills in long-distance ocean voyaging than any other seafaring nation of Europe. They had done this over more than 50 years of voyaging further and further down the west African coast, searching for gold, ivory, and pepper and controlling the whole west African coast for Portugal's profit. But if Portuguese ships were ever to bring home the silks and spices of China, Southeast Asia and India, they would have to reach and cross the seas on the far side of Africa which had been controlled by the Muslims of Arabia for hundreds of years. The perils of the long ocean voyage around Africa would be only the beginning for the first Portuguese sailors who took the sea route to India, which Bartolomeo Diaz had found.

▷ A Portuguese map of 1485, marking the *padroes* set up on the west African coast.

5

The fleet sails

After the return of Diaz from the Indian Ocean in December 1488, nearly ten years passed before Portuguese ships sailed for India. These years were filled with careful preparations for the voyage.

In 1487, along with the ships of Diaz, King John had sent out a daring Portuguese spy, Pero de Covilha. His mission was to travel through the Middle East posing as an Arab, sail to India on an Arab ship, and learn all he could about the Arab shipping routes between the east coast of Africa and India.

After many adventures, Covilha reached the Indian ports of Calicut and Goa, then crossed the sea to east Africa and traveled through the Muslim city-states of east Africa as far south as Sofala – only about 1,600 kilometers (1,000 miles) from the furthest point reached by Diaz. By late 1490 Covilha was back in Cairo, and sent a detailed report of his discoveries to King John in Portugal.

Covilha's report, however, was overtaken almost at once by the arrival in Lisbon (March 1493) of Columbus, home from his first crossing of the Atlantic. He had sailed for the rulers of Spain and

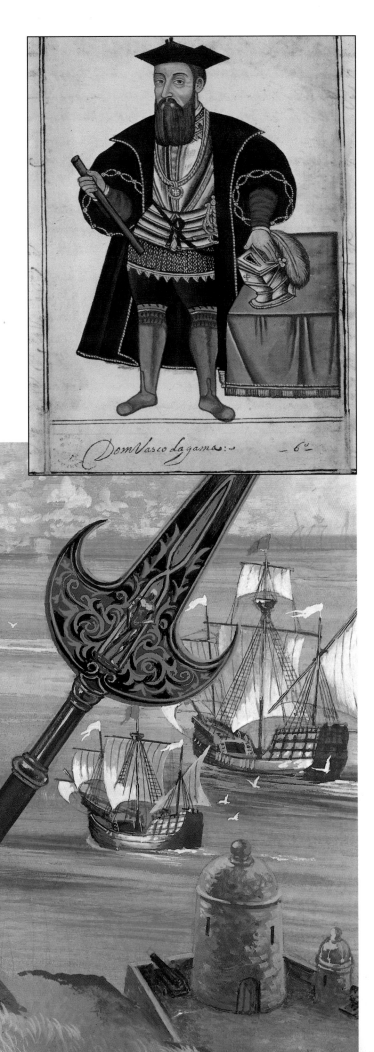

◁ Vasco da Gama was born in 1460 into a proud family of soldiers. He was a man of harsh discipline and a superb leader of men – and, as he proved on the first voyage to India, a master of the new science of ocean navigation.

claimed to have reached the islands of the Indies by traveling westward. After 18 months of arguing, Spain and Portugal agreed on a **Line of Demarcation**, west of which all new discoveries would go to Spain, while the African route to India would be left to Portugal. The treaty line was drawn 370 leagues to the west of the Cape Verde islands. Its modern position would be longitude 50°W. The illness and death of King John of Portugal (1495) caused further delays, but in 1496 the new king, Manuel I, at last ordered a fleet to be prepared for the first voyage to India.

There were four ships in all: two large merchant ships armed with small cannon, the *Sao Gabriel* and *Sao Rafael*; a light caravel, the *Berrio*; and an unnamed storeship. This was loaded with food and drink calculated to last 160 officers and men for three years, and goods for trading once they reached India.

To command the expedition, King Manuel chose the 37-year-old Vasco da Gama, a tough soldier and nobleman who had studied the new science of navigating across the oceans. On July 8, 1497, with all preparations completed, da Gama and his fleet set sail from Lisbon.

◁ To thundering cannon salutes, the blessings of the Church, and the laments of many who feared that the adventurers were sailing to certain death in unknown seas – the four ships of Vasco da Gama's fleet headed down Lisbon's Tagus River for the open sea on July 8, 1497.

The wide Atlantic

▷ Noon in the South Atlantic, and da Gama makes the daily check on the fleet's latitude. He is using the **astrolabe**, peering through the small holes in the swiveling pointer to make sure that this is pointing straight at the sun, whose **altitude** he will then read off from the scale around the astrolabe's rim. A careful navigator, da Gama had a larger wooden astrolabe for taking more accurate readings on solid land than could be made from a ship's unsteady deck.

Da Gama's outward voyage from Portugal to Africa's southern tip was unlike any that had gone before. After leaving the Portuguese **Cape Verde Islands** and heading south across the equator, da Gama did not go on following the line of the African coast. As Cao and Diaz had learned, a current flowing north made progress slow if ships kept too close to the coastline. Instead, da Gama headed boldly out into the South Atlantic, thousands of miles from Africa. This was the longest voyage out of sight of land that any European ship had achieved.

Da Gama was the first sea captain on record to make use of the southeast **trade winds.** These steady, reliable winds of the Southern Hemisphere enabled ships to sail southwest across the South Atlantic until they met the next of the world's wind systems: the **westerlies**, blowing from the South Atlantic into the Indian Ocean. The confidence with which da Gama sailed out into the South Atlantic on August 3, 1497,

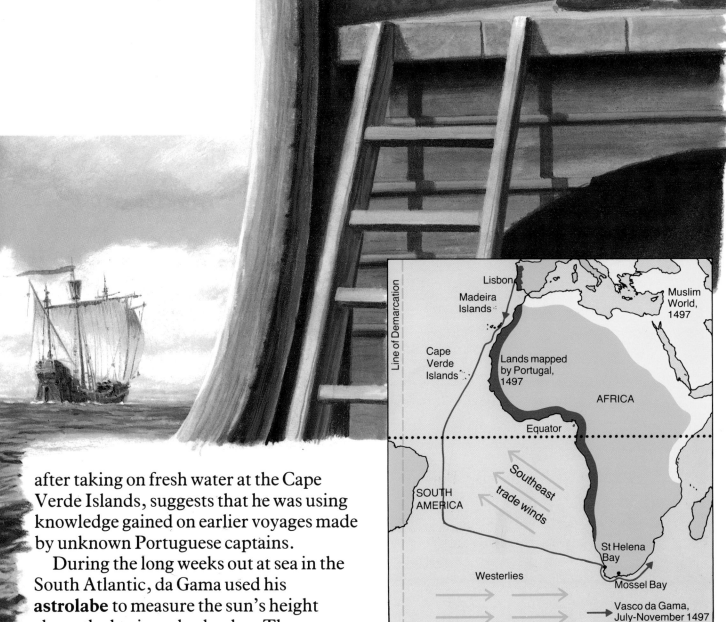

Da Gama's route from the Cape Verde Islands to south Africa: a long haul to the southwest before swinging east toward the African coast.

after taking on fresh water at the Cape Verde Islands, suggests that he was using knowledge gained on earlier voyages made by unknown Portuguese captains.

During the long weeks out at sea in the South Atlantic, da Gama used his **astrolabe** to measure the sun's height above the horizon day by day. These measurements told him how far south of the equator the ships had traveled, their **latitude** south. From the information brought back by Diaz, da Gama already knew the latitude of Africa's southern tip. Once he was far enough south, he could turn east to pass that important landmark, the "Cape of Good Hope" as King John had named it.

At 9 o'clock on the morning of November 4, 1497, da Gama's lookouts sighted the first land seen since the Cape Verde Islands three months before. As the land ran from north to south, da Gama knew that he had turned east too soon; he had reached the African coast about 160

kilometers (100 miles) north of the Cape of Good Hope, which he had planned to pass to the south. Yet, he could be well pleased with his achievement. He had brought his ships and his men safely through a truly wonderful voyage, 13 weeks without sight of land, a record-breaking journey for European sailors. (Columbus, traveling to the west, had been out of sight of land for only seven weeks during his famous first crossing of the Atlantic, five years earlier.)

9

On the threshold

When he reached the African coast after the long voyage south from the Cape Verde Islands, da Gama's first need was for a safe anchorage where his ships could be overhauled and repaired after so many weeks at sea. This he found at Saint Helena Bay, about 128 kilometers (80 miles) north of modern Cape Town.

At Saint Helena Bay the ships were carefully run ashore, at a point where they could be refloated at high tide. They were emptied of their stores and **careened** – heeled over so that the underside of their hulls was exposed for **breaming** (burning off growths of seaweed) and **caulking** (plugging leaky seams between planks). While this work was in progress, the Portuguese had the first European encounter with the inhabitants of south Africa; the **Hottentots**.

At first the Hottentots seemed friendly enough, accepting the bells and rings which the Portuguese gave them as presents. But the Hottentots were not the "men of little spirit, quite incapable of violence" the Portuguese mistakenly took them to be. When one of da Gama's officers tried to walk in on a Hottentot village without being invited, the villagers angrily drove him away with their fishing spears, and in the ensuing fight da Gama himself was jabbed in the leg.

When all repairs were finished, the fleet sailed from Saint Helena Bay on November 16, rounded the Cape of Good Hope on the 22nd and sailed on to Mossel Bay, about halfway between modern Cape Town and Port Elizabeth. Here, da Gama called another halt. Before he passed the furthest point reached by Diaz and pushed on into the unknown, he wanted to rearrange his ships' crews and their stocks of food and water.

While the Portuguese rested at Mossel Bay, at what was for them the threshold of the known world, they had their second encounter with the Hottentots. Da Gama took an armed party ashore, but no force was needed. The Hottentots willingly traded one of their oxen for three bracelets, and played on their flute-like *gorahs* for the Portuguese – the first concert of African music recorded by Europeans.

◁ Encounter at the southern end of the known world: a Hottentot huntsman watches da Gama's men at work in Saint Helena Bay, breaming and caulking their ships. The Portuguese were surprised at how similar the Hottentots' hunting dogs were to the dogs of Portugal, noting that even their barking sounded the same!

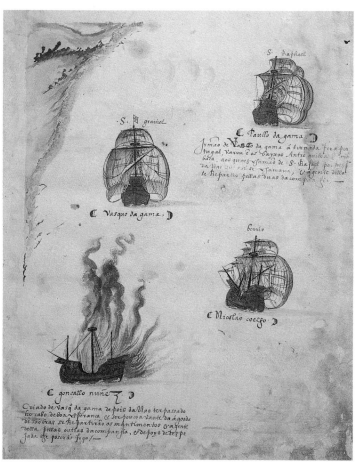

△ A Portuguese book shows da Gama's three ships sailing on after the burning of the storeship.

▷ On the beach at the Mossel Bay anchorage, da Gama's crewmen prepare to ferry out another load of provisions casks, spare spars, timber, and metal fittings from the abandoned storeship to the ships out in the bay.

Burning the storeship

When the fleet left Mossel Bay, it would be heading into uncharted waters. There was every chance that the ships might lose touch with each other in bad weather. (Just such an accident had separated the two ships of Columbus, *Niña* and *Pinta*, during their voyage home across the Atlantic in 1493; each thought the other had sunk.) If this happened it was vital for each ship to have the strongest possible crew, and good food supplies, to have the best chance of reaching home if it could not find the other ships of the scattered

fleet.

To make sure of this, da Gama chose the Mossel Bay anchorage as the place to empty the storeship, cram her stores into the holds of *Sao Gabriel*, *Sao Rafael*, and *Berrio*, and share out the storeship's crew between those of the other three ships. The storeship itself was stripped of every spar, rope, timber, and metal fitting which might be needed by the others for repairs in the future. Once this had been done, the empty hulk of the storeship was burned.

In December 1497, the voyage was resumed, with all eyes now scanning the African shoreline for what, to the Portuguese, was the frontier of the known world: the *padrao* marker set up by Diaz when he turned for home in 1488. After this was passed, da Gama knew that the fleet must make all speed to reach the southernmost Muslim ports reported by Covilha before provisions ran dangerously low. On Christmas Day 1497, in honor of the "Natal Day," or birthday of Christ, da Gama gave the name "Natal" to the coast they were passing. But progress was slowed by the Mozambique Current, flowing southwest between the island of Madagascar and the African mainland, and steering further out to sea did not help them go faster.

By the end of January, da Gama had to reduce the men's daily water ration to less than one-third of a liter (three-quarters of a pint) per day, and order the salt beef to be cooked in seawater. By the beginning of March it had taken da Gama's fleet more than three weary, thirst-parched months to sail 2,740 kilometers (1,700 miles) around the southeastern corner of Africa.

The sultan's anger

▷ The course followed by da Gama along the east African coast. He sailed from Mozambique to the friendly port of Malindi, northeast of Mombasa.

▷ ▷ The first town sighted in seven months at sea: da Gama's officers gaze at the colorful scene on the waterfront at Mozambique, where spreading sunshades shield important Muslim officials from the heat of the sun. At Mozambique, the hostility of the sultan and his scornful refusal to accept the trade goods brought in the Portuguese ships was an unwelcome surprise for da Gama.

AFRICA

Malindi
Mombasa

Mozambique
Sofala

NATAL

St Helena Bay
Cape of Good Hope
Mossel Bay

By the middle of February 1498, the slow crawl along Africa's southeast coast had taken so long that da Gama had been forced to land at a river mouth to take on fresh water. A split in *Sao Rafael's* mainmast also needed repairing. But at last, on March 2, 1498, da Gama and his men sighted the white buildings, mosque domes, and slim minarets of the first town they had seen since leaving the Cape Verde Islands, 15,000 kilometers (9,320 miles) away in the Atlantic.

This was the Muslim trading port of Mozambique, from which the modern country takes its name. It lay 900 kilometers (560 miles) northeast of the southernmost Muslim port on the east African coast, Sofala, which da Gama had unknowingly passed out at sea, and 3,000

kilometers (1,860 miles) from Mossel Bay.

Da Gama's orders from King Manuel of Portugal were to get on good terms with the Muslim sultans of east Africa, in order to open the whole coast to Portuguese trade. But at Mozambique the Portuguese found that the trade goods they had brought – the trinkets, beads, and little bells which pleased west coast Africans and the Hottentots of the south – were regarded as cheap rubbish by the east coast Muslim merchants. The sultan of Mozambique rejected all the goods that da Gama showed him, and scornfully refused to trade. The Portuguese were only able to buy a few goats and pigeons in the market in exchange for their glass beads, and da Gama decided to sail on in the hope of finding better luck up the coast.

When the Portuguese ships reached Mombasa, 1,290 kilometers (800 miles) north of Mozambique, it did seem for a brief moment that their luck had changed. As they approached the harbor, they saw that all the ships there were dressed with colorful flags, as if in welcome. But this was not in honor of the Portuguese arrival. It was the Muslim feast of **Eid**, celebrating the end of **Ramadan**, the month of fasting, and the Christian ships were far from welcome. Although the sultan of Mombasa sent friendly messages to da Gama, offering to allow the Portuguese to trade for spices, his real intention was to lure the Portuguese ships inside the harbor and capture them in a surprise attack.

The Portuguese were alerted to the danger by a lucky accident. The ships were heading into the inner harbor, on the morning of April 10, three days after their arrival in sight of Mombasa, when two of them clumsily ran into each other. When da Gama ordered the fleet to anchor again for repairs to be made, the Muslims who had come on board to guide the ships in jumped overboard and were picked up by a boat waiting alongside. Suspecting treachery, da Gama tortured the truth out of two other Muslim captives by dropping boiling oil on their skin. That same night (August 10) two boats filled with armed Muslim men approached, sending swimmers who tried to cut the ships' anchor cables before they were spotted by the Portuguese lookouts. There was nothing to do but leave Mombasa and sail on.

Departure from Malindi

Malindi, the third Muslim port visited by da Gama's fleet on the east African coast, was only 100 kilometers (62 miles) north of Mombasa, but here the reception that greeted the Portuguese could not have been more different. The sultan of Malindi was an enemy of his rival down the coast at Mombasa, and welcomed the Portuguese as possible allies. In exchange for da Gama's cheap trade goods, the sultan sent generous gifts of food and quantities of the Far Eastern spices most valued by the Europeans: cloves, cumin, ginger, nutmeg, and pepper. The sultan also told da Gama that he would gladly provide what da Gama needed most of all: skilled **pilots** to guide the Portuguese across the Indian Ocean to India. During their nine-day stay at Malindi (April 15-24, 1498), the Portuguese met their first Indians. These were sailors, from the northwestern Indian district of Gujarat, and they spoke enough Arabic to be able to talk with the Portuguese. They were not Muslims, and seemed to pay respect to an image of the Virgin Mary that they were shown. This made da Gama believe they were Christians. They were really Hindus, a religion then unknown to Europeans.

△ Nearly 500 years after da Gama's ships dropped anchor there, a mosque in Mombasa shows that Muslim influence along the east coast of Africa is still a powerful force in the region.

"They told us that they ate no beef," one of the Portuguese noted.

Malindi reminded the Portuguese of a town in their own country. Its houses were lofty and well whitewashed, and had many windows; on the land side were palm groves, and all around corn and vegetables were being cultivated.

However, on da Gama's orders, his men stayed on their guard throughout their visit. With memories of Mozambique and Mombasa, da Gama refused to go ashore at Malindi; he and the sultan did their talking from boats. But at last the sultan sent "a Christian pilot," and the fleet sailed for India on April 22.

◁ Parley at the quayside. At Malindi, despite the friendly reception offered to him and his men, da Gama refused to risk going ashore in case of treachery. He talked with the sultan of Malindi from the safety of his ship.

17

India at last

Da Gama's luck had held good again. The "Christian pilot" provided by the sultan of Malindi was the most famous Asian navigator of his time, the Gujarati seaman Ahmad ibn Majid. He had written a set of **sailing instructions** for the Indian Ocean (the *Al Mahet*) that were much used by Arab sailors.

With the expert guidance of ibn Majid, da Gama's fleet crossed the Indian Ocean in 23 days, avoiding the dangerous coral reefs of the **Laccadive Islands**, to sight the coast of India on May 18, 1498. Two days later, they experienced their first **monsoon** storm at sea. The diarist wrote, "Owing to the heavy rain and a thunderstorm, which prevailed while we were sailing along the coast, our pilot was unable to identify the exact locality." But then the weather cleared, and ibn Majid sighted landmarks which he knew well. At last, on May 20, 1498, da Gama's ships anchored off the Indian port of Calicut.

At Calicut, the Arab influence was strong. The first men they met were Arabs from the western Mediterranean sea who could speak Italian, Spanish and Portuguese. "A lucky venture!" one of these Arabs told the Portuguese. "Plenty of rubies, plenty of emeralds! You owe great thanks to God, for having brought you to a country holding such riches!"

But it was not to be. The Zamorin,

Calicut's Hindu ruler, greeted da Gama but was insulted by the cheap gifts and poor trade goods he received. He refused to offend the wealthy Arab merchants, who paid generously for the rich trade of India, by giving special terms to the newcomers. The Zamorin agreed to sell da Gama food, but no more.

Prevented from proper trading, da Gama told his men to exchange what they could in the Calicut markets, and so built up a modest cargo of spices and jewels. But by August 1498, as he prepared to leave, da Gama knew that future trade with India could only be carried out if the Portuguese used force.

▷ Indian boats swarm around the Portuguese ships in Calicut harbor, offering welcome fresh fruit and vegetables for sale. Food was the only item that the Zamorin of Calicut would agree to sell to da Gama.

▷ An early view of the city and harbor of Calicut at the time of da Gama's arrival in May 1498.

Agony in the Indian Ocean

On August 29, 1498, da Gama's ships set sail from Calicut on their long voyage home to Portugal. Although the sea passage from Europe to India had been proved possible, da Gama's main mission of establishing peaceful trade with India had ended in failure. He headed north up the Indian coast in the hope of finding a more friendly port where trading terms might be more favorable, but without success. At the end of September 1498, he ordered the ships to be beached, careened, and caulked before beginning the return voyage in mid-October.

This time, however, da Gama did not have the expert guidance of pilot Ahmad ibn Majid. He was also attempting the east–west crossing of the Indian Ocean at the worst season of the year, when instead of steady following winds the ships had to endure alternating calms and headwinds. As a result, it took them three months to complete a crossing which had taken only 23 days on the outward voyage.

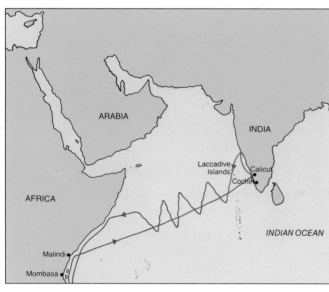

△ Across the Indian Ocean. The uncertain track of the return crossing to the African coast, caused by unfavorable weather, was very different from the rapid outward crossing from Malindi to Calicut.

▷ The crew of da Gama's flagship *Sao Gabriel* during the terrible return crossing of the Indian Ocean, October-December 1498, when 30 crewmen died of the disease scurvy.

It was a dreadful ordeal. As the fresh water and food ran out, the men suffered increasingly not only from thirst but from **scurvy**, the disease caused by lack of Vitamin C on long ocean voyages. As the men grew weaker, their limbs became swollen and blackened; their teeth loosened in their rotting gums, which oozed black blood. Too weak to work, or even to fight off the rats which gnawed at their feet where they lay, they gradually began to die. By the time the weakened survivors sighted the African coast again in January 1499, 30 of their fellow sailors had died and been buried at sea. "I assure you," wrote the unknown diarist who wrote the only surviving account of the voyage, "that if the state of affairs had continued for another fortnight, there would have been no men at all to navigate the ships."

Luckily for his men, da Gama had escaped the worst effects of scurvy. His excellent navigation brought them back again to Malindi. Here the sultan generously supplied the feeble Portuguese crews with fresh meat, eggs, and above all fruit, the best and quickest cure for scurvy. But even when all those still able to do so had regained their health, there were not enough survivors to man all three ships. Da Gama therefore ordered the *Sao Rafael* to be abandoned and burned, keeping only the beautiful wooden statue of the Archangel Rafael, the ship's guardian angel. *Sao Rafael*'s crewmen were then shared out between *Sao Gabriel* and *Berrio* before the ships headed south for the Cape of Good Hope and the Atlantic Ocean.

Return to Portugal

Remembering the hostility of the sultans of Mombasa and Mozambique during the outward voyage, da Gama avoided both ports on his run to the Cape of Good Hope, which was rounded in March 1499. But the two ships with their weakened crews were still more than 11,000 kilometers (6,800 miles) from home, and the long voyage north inevitably saw further deaths caused by scurvy and other diseases.

One of the many victims was da Gama's own brother Paulo, former captain of the *Sao Rafael* until it was abandoned at Malindi. Paulo was already gravely ill when they rounded the Cape of Good Hope, and by the time the ships reached the Cape Verde Islands in May he was beyond recovery. When Vasco da Gama realized that his brother would die long before Portugal was reached, he steered for the islands of the **Azores** owned by Portugal, so that Paulo could at least receive a Christian burial. In memory of his dead brother, Vasco da Gama kept the statue from *Sao Rafael* for the rest of his life.

The ships returned to Portugal some time between August 29 and September 1, 1499; the exact date is not known. Da Gama's voyage had been paid for with heavy loss of life among his crews.

When *Sao Gabriel* and *Berrio* finally dropped anchor off Lisbon in September 1499, only 54 men were still alive out of the 160 with whom da Gama had set out 26 months before. In their journey to India and back they had made the longest voyage in the history of the world: 43,440 kilometers (27,000 miles) – enough to have sailed right around the world, if they had

only known.

King Manuel was overjoyed with da Gama's achievement. For the past six years, thanks to the discoveries of Columbus, Spain had led the field in world exploration. But Columbus had found only islands; da Gama had sailed to the mainland of Asia, whose trade Portugal now had only to reach out and take.

◁ The city and port of Lisbon as it looked 400 years ago. It was the starting point for many great voyages of exploration.

▽ On September 18, 1499, da Gama and his gallant survivors parade with their banners through the packed and cheering streets of Lisbon.

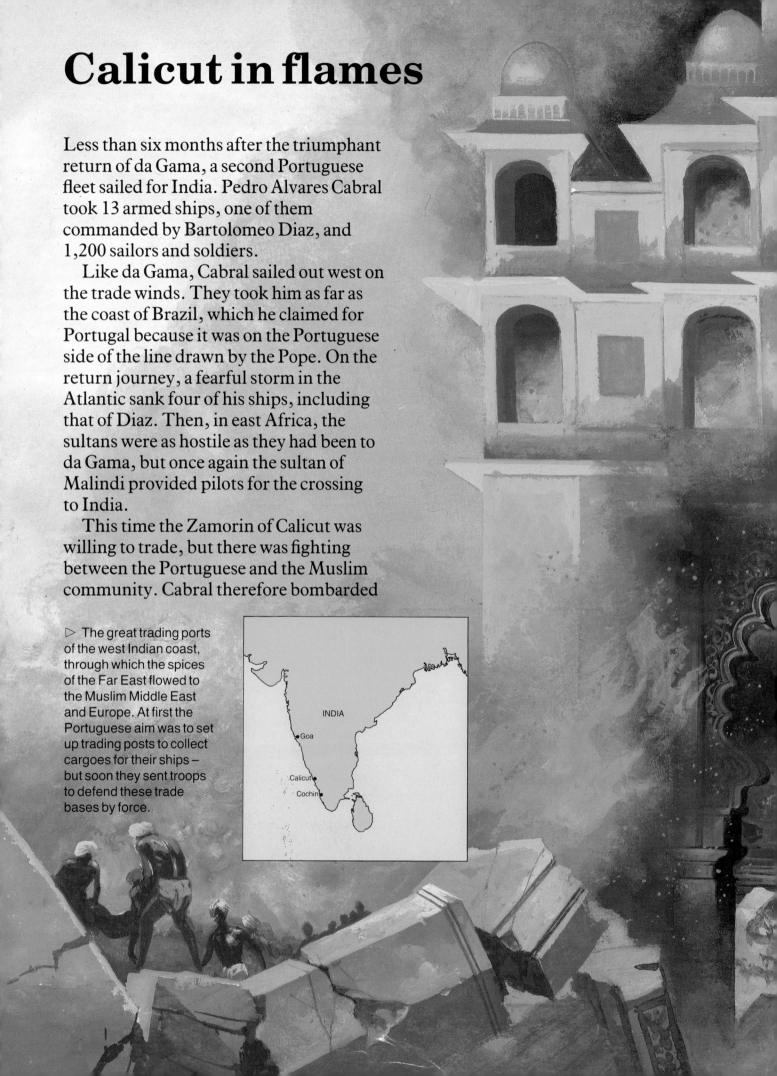

Calicut in flames

Less than six months after the triumphant return of da Gama, a second Portuguese fleet sailed for India. Pedro Alvares Cabral took 13 armed ships, one of them commanded by Bartolomeo Diaz, and 1,200 sailors and soldiers.

Like da Gama, Cabral sailed out west on the trade winds. They took him as far as the coast of Brazil, which he claimed for Portugal because it was on the Portuguese side of the line drawn by the Pope. On the return journey, a fearful storm in the Atlantic sank four of his ships, including that of Diaz. Then, in east Africa, the sultans were as hostile as they had been to da Gama, but once again the sultan of Malindi provided pilots for the crossing to India.

This time the Zamorin of Calicut was willing to trade, but there was fighting between the Portuguese and the Muslim community. Cabral therefore bombarded

▷ The great trading ports of the west Indian coast, through which the spices of the Far East flowed to the Muslim Middle East and Europe. At first the Portuguese aim was to set up trading posts to collect cargoes for their ships – but soon they sent troops to defend these trade bases by force.

INDIA

Goa

Calicut

Cochin

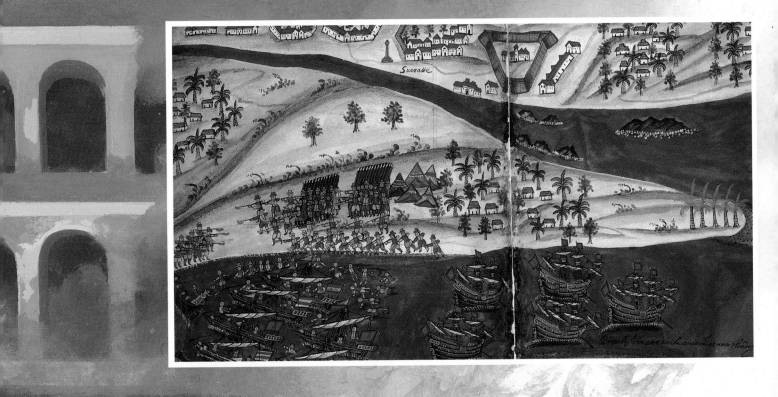

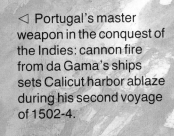

◁ Portugal's master weapon in the conquest of the Indies: cannon fire from da Gama's ships sets Calicut harbor ablaze during his second voyage of 1502-4.

△ An early European foothold in India. The Indian port of Surat, north of modern Bombay, had been built up into a defended Portuguese colony by 1646.

Calicut with his ships' guns before moving south to Cochin. Here he loaded a rich cargo of spices and was allowed to build a trading post, or **factory,** before sailing for home, which he reached in 1501.

Command of the third Portuguese voyage to India (1502-4) was given to da Gama again: a powerful fleet of 20 armed ships. This was not a peaceful trading mission, but the first attempt to break Muslim unwillingness to trade by force. Da Gama's ferocious bombardment of Calicut forced the Zamorin to guarantee the safety of the trading post set up by Cabral at Cochin. From now on, the Portuguese would fight to the death to control the trade of India.

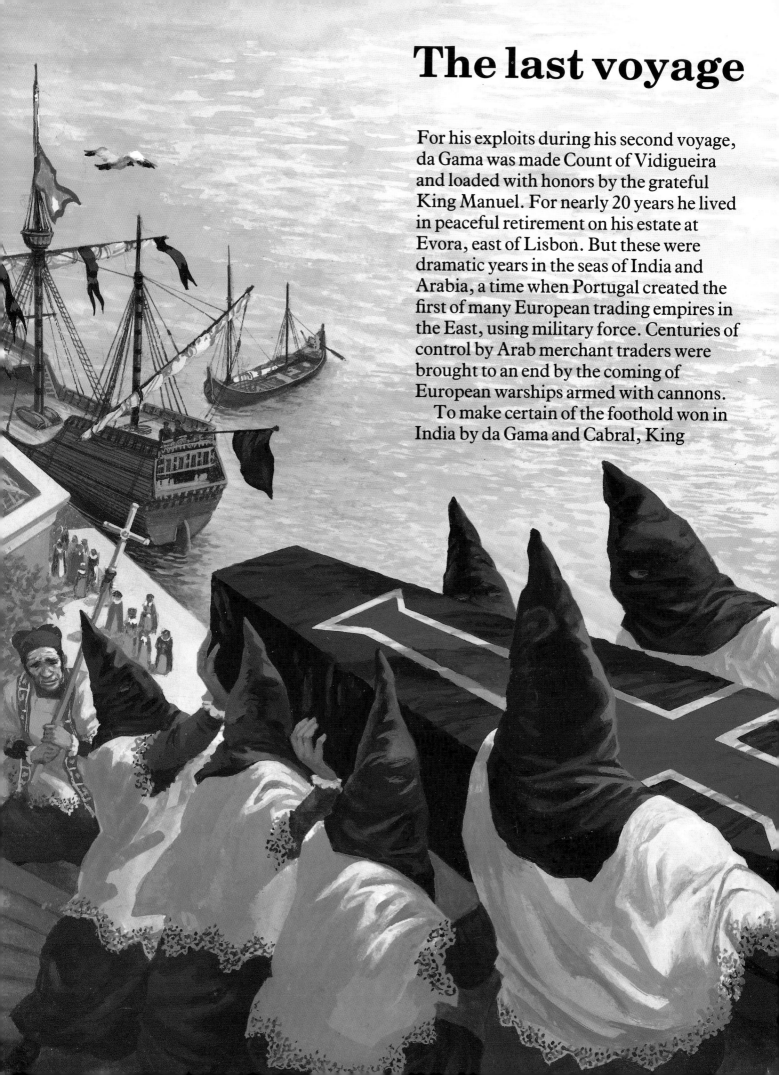

The last voyage

For his exploits during his second voyage, da Gama was made Count of Vidigueira and loaded with honors by the grateful King Manuel. For nearly 20 years he lived in peaceful retirement on his estate at Evora, east of Lisbon. But these were dramatic years in the seas of India and Arabia, a time when Portugal created the first of many European trading empires in the East, using military force. Centuries of control by Arab merchant traders were brought to an end by the coming of European warships armed with cannons.

To make certain of the foothold won in India by da Gama and Cabral, King

Manuel sent out two powerful "Viceroys of India": Francesco d'Almeida (1505-9) and Affonso d'Albuquerque (1509-15). In repeated battles, their fleets destroyed the Muslim trading empire which da Gama had first entered in 1498. The hostile sultanates on the east African coast were conquered and turned into staging areas for Portuguese shipping. Goa, captured by Albuquerque in 1510, became Portugal's most powerful base on the west Indian coast and the longest-lived European colony in Asia. They conquered Hormuz at the mouth of the Persian Gulf, and Malacca in Malaya. These gains gave Portugal total control of the all-important spice trade. King Manuel "The Fortunate" added to his other titles that of "Lord of the Commerce of Ethiopia, Arabia, Persia, and India." Envious European rulers sourly called him the "Grocer King."

By the time King Manuel died in 1521, there were many complaints of the cruelty and greed of the Portuguese using the King's service in the East as a chance to get rich quick. Da Gama was called from retirement and appointed Viceroy by King John III, but died on December 24, 1524, shortly after landing at Cochin, at the age of 64.

◁ After resting at Cochin since his death in 1524, Vasco da Gama's coffin is reverently embarked in 1531 for the long voyage home to Portugal. There the Viceroy's body was reburied on his main estate at Vidigueira, but in 1898 it was transferred to the magnificent Church of the Jeronimos at Belem.

△ The tomb of da Gama lies in the Church of the Jeronimos. This church, at the mouth of the Tagus River, was built by King Manuel in thanks for da Gama's first voyage to India.

New empire in the east

Vasco da Gama was not only a great seaman and navigator who achieved one of the greatest and most important voyages of the Age of Exploration. He was also one of the founders of the first of the European trade empires which dominated the history of the world for the next four and a half centuries, until their break up after World War II.

Within 20 years of da Gama's return to Portugal from his first voyage to India in 1497-1499, the Portuguese had broken the Arab control of sea trade with Asia that had endured for 500 years. First under Almeida, then under Albuquerque, Portuguese sea power in Asian waters was extended from west India eastward to Malacca. In 1513, the Portuguese Jorge Alvarez was the first European to reach China by sea. Within 18 years of da Gama's death, in 1542, Antonio da Mota had reached Japan.

The direct sea link with the **Spice Islands**, the Molucca Islands in the East Indies, briefly gave Portugal total control of the spice trade. In 1519, this was challenged by a Portuguese sailor, Ferdinand Magellan. He had fought bravely for Portugal at Malacca in 1509, survived a shipwreck in the Indian Ocean, and had been wounded in battle against the Muslims of Morocco in 1512. But Magellan was later treated ungratefully by King Manuel, and left Portugal in anger. In 1517 Magellan decided to take service with the king of Spain. He sailed west to cross the Pacific Ocean and reach the Spice Islands from the east – so bringing about the first sea voyage to complete the circuit of the world (1519-22).

◁ An enduring monument to Portugal's trading empire in the East: a Catholic church in Goa, the port on the west coast of India conquered by da Gama's successor Affonso d'Albuquerque, in 1510. Goa became the first European colony in Asia – and was one of the last to go. It remained a colony of Portugal until 1962, when the city became part of the Republic of India.

▷ The spread of Portugal's trading empire, eastward from India to Malacca and the Spice Islands in the East Indies; north and east to China and Japan.

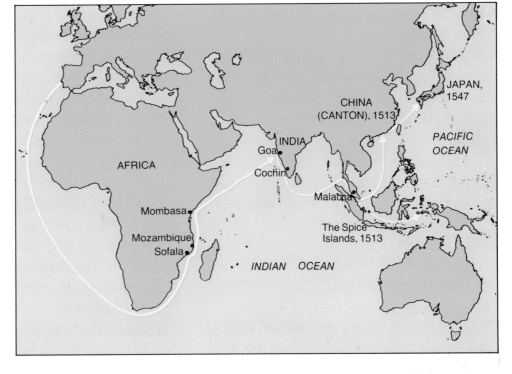

▽ The most prized of all the spices, and the most costly: cloves, from the Moluccan islands of Ternate and Tidore, first reached by Portuguese ships in 1513.

Glossary

Altitude The height of the sun or a star above the horizon.

Astrolabe Navigator's instrument for measuring the altitude of the sun or a star, to calculate the ship's latitude.

Azores Atlantic island group about 1,450 kilometers (about 800 miles) west of Portugal; discovered in 1427-31.

Breaming Heating weeds and barnacles on the underside of a beached ship, so that they can be scraped off.

Cape Verde Islands Atlantic island group about 640 kilometers (400 miles) west of Senegal, Africa; discovered in 1456.

Caravel Small, three or four-masted sailing ship, used on all major voyages of exploration from about 1420-1510.

Careening To beach a ship on its side for cleaning or repairing the hull.

Caulking Hammering waterproof material, or pouring hot pitch, into the seams between planks to stop leaks.

Demarcation, Line of Imaginary line drawn north and south down the Atlantic Ocean. Lands to the east of the line were granted to Portugal, lands to the west of the line to Spain.

Eid Muslim festival celebrating the end of Ramadan, the month of fasting.

Factory Trading post in a foreign country with a warehouse for storing goods for shipping (run by a "factor").

Hottentots Inhabitants of south Africa; most were ousted by Dutch settlers and Bantu Africans by about 1800.

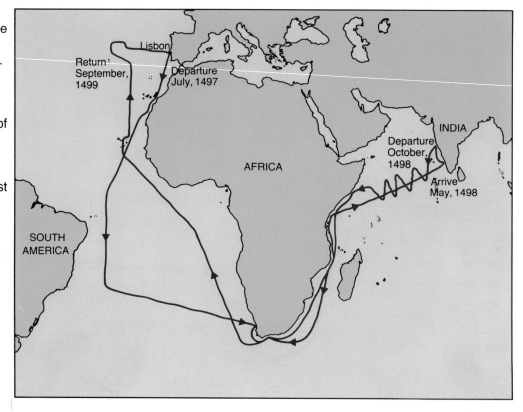

▷ Vasco da Gama's greatest achievement: the first sea voyage from Europe to India and back. Although his success owed much to the knowledge gained by the seafarers and explorers of earlier years, it was the most important ocean voyage made before Ferdinand Magellan's first crossing of the Pacific Ocean in 1520-1521. Before da Gama, no European sailor had steered so far and for so long from the nearest land, confidently relying on ocean winds to take him to places he had never seen. Only an expert captain and navigator could have done it.

Timechart

Laccadive Islands Group of coral islands in the Arabian Sea, about 300 kilometers (200 miles) off the southwest coast of India.

Latitude Measurement of position north or south of the equator.

Monsoon Seasonal winds and heavy rains caused by the summer heating, and winter cooling, of the land mass of Asia.

Padrao (plural, *padroes*) Portuguese word for a stone marker column topped by a cross.

Pilot Expert navigator taken aboard a ship to guide the captain.

Ramadan The Muslim holy month of fasting, when for 30 days Muslims eat and drink nothing from dawn to sunset.

Sailing instructions Detailed written information about local winds, tides and currents, plus bearings and distances from port to port.

Scurvy Disease caused by lack of Vitamin C on long ocean voyages, in the years when fresh fruit and vegetables could not be preserved.

Spice Islands The islands of Ternate and Tidore in the Moluccas, East Indies, where the clove spice grows naturally.

Trade winds Steady winds, caused in the atmosphere by Earth's spin, which blow toward the equator from the northeast in the Northern Hemisphere (northeast trades) and from the southeast in the Southern Hemisphere (southeast trades).

Westerlies Strong winds that blow from west to east around Earth's Southern Hemisphere.

1460 Vasco da Gama is born in Portugal.

1487-88 Bartolomeo Diaz of Portugal rounds the Cape of Good Hope and enters the Indian Ocean.

1492 Christopher Columbus, in Spanish service, crosses the Atlantic and discovers the West Indies.

1494 Pope Alexander VI divides the world outside Europe between Spain (the west) and Portugal (the east).

July 1497 Da Gama sails from Portugal for India with four ships.

December 1497 Da Gama passes the furthest point reached by Diaz.

March 1498 Da Gama reaches Mozambique on Africa's east coast.

May 1498 Da Gama reaches Calicut in India.

September 1498 Da Gama sails from India for Africa and home.

March 1499 Da Gama rounds the Cape of Good Hope and re-enters the Atlantic.

September 1499 Da Gama returns to Portugal.

1500-1502 Voyage of Pedro Alvares Cabral to India and back.

1502-4 Second voyage of da Gama to India and back.

1510 Portuguese capture Goa in India.

1513 First Portuguese ships reach China and the Spice Islands.

1519-21 Ferdinand Magellan, in Spanish service, dies during first voyage around the world.

December 1524 Vasco da Gama dies at Cochin, India.

Index